Reading Race,
Reading the Bible

FACETS

Selected Titles in the Facets Series

Reading Race, Reading the Bible

Peter T. Nash

Fortress Press
Minneapolis

READING RACE, READING THE BIBLE

Cover art: *Sheets of Paper* © Tommy Flynn/Photonica
Book design: Joseph Bonyata

ISBN 0-8006-3633-3

The paper used in this publication meets the minimum requirements of American National Standard for Information Sciences — Permanence of Paper for Printed Library Materials, ANSI Z329.48-1984.

Manufactured in the U.S.A.
07 06 05 04 03 1 2 3 4 5 6 7 8 9 10

for Jack[†] and Marion,
who taught me about the damage that the ideas
of race do to us all

for Will,[†]
who taught me about the damage that race does
in and through the church

for Carrie, Theo, Simon, and Tobias,
in hopes of sharing with them a world in which
life is valued by the quality of love one gives and
receives, rather than the chromosomes of those
who live and love

Contents

Acknowledgments

I am obliged to enough people for enough reasons for the research and production of this book that another chapter would be warranted. First, thanks go to the students and colleagues at Escola Superior de Teologia (EST) and O Instituto Ecumênico de Pós Graduacão em São Leopoldo who taught me much over the past eight years, especially the members of the *grupo identidade,* who shared with me the road to identifying the bankrupt practice of categorizing human beings into races and using that concept to divide people and hoard power and wealth. I also owe a special thanks to the institution itself and its director, Lothar Hoch. In 1999 he invited me to renew my contract at EST with an alteration that would give me a reduced teaching load so as to allow me to dedicate 50 percent of my time to research and administrative tasks on the subject of *Negritude na Bíblia e na Igreja*—blackness in the Bible and the church. In 2001 my colleagues in the department of biblical studies and faculty representatives approved my study-leave to work on this and other parts of the project.

In the second semester of 2001 I was graciously received by Professor Dieter Becker, who was the Rektor at Augustana Theologische Hochschule in Neuendettelsau. At Augustana, Professor Wolfgang Stegemann was patient and generous with his time and resources, including photocopying and allowing his very apt secretary, Andrea Siebert, to assist me with many of the details of living and researching in Germany that I could not have handled on my own. While Professor Stegemann can be credited with encouraging me to think in anthropological terms about the African presence in the Old Testament, he cannot be faulted for errors of method that one may find here. There are many more to thank for meaningful contributions to my time at Augustana: Dr. Christian Strecker, Professor Helmut Utzschneider, Dr. Renate Jost, and Mr. Armin Stephan and Mr. Markus Bomba and their exceptional and attentive library staff, along with the students, complete the essentials.

Being in Germany also presented the opportunity to test some ideas with colleagues and their graduate students and the general public in two cases. Two groups at the University of Lund were kind enough to give me time and feedback; Manfred and Christina Hofmann and Tryggve Mettinger opened their classrooms. At Philipps-Universität in Marburg, Emeritus Professor Erhard Gerstenberger arranged with Professors Jörg Jeremias and Rainer Kessler for me to test ideas in a session of their graduate Old Testament seminar. That seminar raised several issues that improved the quality of my research in general, in most cases only indirectly in this essay, but Dr. Gerlinde Baumann was especially helpful in pointing out the possible connections between African and Old Testament proverbial traditions that Claus Westermann had begun to acknowledge might bear fruit. In Erlangen, Professor Walter Sparn was kind enough to cede a Tuesday afternoon with his graduate seminar in systematic theology, in which he and the graduate students raised issues that had been raised at the University of Oslo where Kjetil Hafsted and Notto Thelle allowed me to present and debate issues of the Old Testament and Africa with a master's level seminar on contextual theology. For this last opportunity, I thank the International Network of Advanced Theological Education.

In terms of financial support, the Division for Global Ministry (DGM) of the Evangelical Lutheran Church in America bore the onus for most of my research time. For all but eighteen months of my employment with DGM and during all of the research opportunities, including a period of reassignment to Germany, the Right Reverend Rafael Malpica made it possible for me to move freely among my peers and be challenged to think more broadly about the diversity of contexts in which the Old Testament is read. He conspired with our mutual friend and mentor, the Right Reverend Will Herzfeld, to send me to Brazil in 1995 as part of DGM's commitment to work for racial justice in the Lutheran communion in churches in environments that offered that possibility. It was Will's vision of a truly global community of Christian sisters and brothers that took me to Brazil and kept me there until after his death in May 2002.

I am also indebted to the students and staff of the Ecumenical Theological Seminary at Ricatla, Mozambique, especially the second-, third-, and fourth-year classes of 1999. It was these students who told me how they saw their families' patterns in the family stories of the Old Testament and prodded me to ask questions about why North Atlantic biblical interpreters do not hear Africa calling out from the Old Testament. Leslie Milton was the academic director who minded me from beginning to end, and the rector, Jonas Ngomane, showed the extraordinary hospitality of lodging me in his home.

Another group that bears mentioning is the Egyptologists who encouraged me, corrected me, and filled my head with data. Two are former classmates from Chicago—Lisa Heidorn, who came to focus on the new materials from the Nubians, and Ann Macy Roth, who seeks to build bridges in the formerly isolated conversations among Egyptologists and Africanists, both professional and militant. A third is Mogens Jørgensen of the Ny Carlsberg Glyptotek, who kindly took a call from a total stranger, became interested in the project, and gave me hours of his time explaining some fine points of Egyptian art.

Penultimately, no book comes to press without the hard work of editors. I am grateful to K. C. Hanson and Beth Wright at Fortress Press for pushing me, following up, and making this contribution come to fruition.

Finally, I thank Jette, with whom I am fortunate to share every minute of life, even when we are apart, and Carrie, Theo, Simon, and Tobias, who complete our joy and make work meaningful.

1
Talking about Race

It is imperative in science to doubt; it is absolutely necessary, for progress in science, to have uncertainty as a fundamental part of your inner nature. To make progress in understanding, we must remain modest and allow that we do not know. Nothing is certain or proved beyond all doubt. You investigate for curiosity, because it is *unknown,* not because you know the answer. And as you develop more information in the sciences, it is not that you are finding out the truth, but that you are finding out that this or that is more or less likely.[1]

In August of 1995 I accepted an invitation to teach at Escola Superior de Teologia in São Leopoldo in Rio Grande do Sul/Brazil. I boarded the plane in Chicago, and anyone who cared to look on saw an African American man boarding the airplane. Earlier in my life I had been Negro, colored, and Black, but in 1995 I was an African American. The multiple identities that I had imagined were behind me would come back to haunt me throughout my work in Brazil. When I arrived at my temporary home and language school in São Paulo, the southernmost of those states that are not a part of the "South" of Brazil, I told my new acquaintances that my employment would include two foci: the field associated with my formal graduate education, Semitic Languages and Hebrew Bible, and, as I gained more familiarity with Brazilian culture, the question of race and racialism and the inclusion of Afro-Brazilians in the IECLB (the Brazilian Lutheran Church that holds membership in the Lutheran World Federation). Several Brazilians were surprised and asked why that interested me. The question was asked again and again until the director of the school laughed and told me, But you are not Black, you are a *"Negro Paraguaio." Paraguaio* in Brazil is slang for "counterfeit goods"—watches with name brands like Folex, running shoes named ReBok, and of course the famous

Japanese brand of consumer electronics, SOMY, a name that has become synonymous with cutting edge technology in your home today and in your trashcan the day after tomorrow. In Brazil, I would learn, I am often not Black. When I am north of the three southernmost states, and depending on the social class within which I am conducting myself, I am most often *Moreno,* a term that serves to describe both the brunettes of European descent and the fairer brown-skinned people. I am sometimes *mulato,* a term used to designate middle brown-toned people almost always indicating some obviously African facial traits. Sometimes, I am—before I open my mouth and my accent betrays me—just plain *Brasileiro.* This last term is used as praise or derision, depending on the situation. As the reader can already see, the racialization of Brazil is quite different from the stark pattern of Black and White in the United States.[2]

We often use the same words to describe different realities. It is not enough to simply know that ideas about racial categories vary from culture to culture. In 1996 I attended an academic conference in Zimbabwe. I arrived two days before the conference began; I scouted around the city of Bulawayo, bought Christmas gifts, and made some acquaintances. I was surprised to learn that sixteen years after the end of Rhodesian apartheid the distinctions between "coloreds" and "Blacks" continued in everyday life. An acquaintance, who very easily could have been mistaken for a member of my family, shocked me with the words, "I hate the Blacks; they have taken over everything." When I protested that I was Black, I was promptly told that for Zimbabweans, I was "foreign colored." Flying out via the Republic of South Africa, I was prepared to be Black for my Christmas in the States. In 1999 I returned to southern Africa, to Mozambique, to teach. Nearing the end of my course, I performed my traveler's duties and bought presents for family and friends. When I complained to my students that I had paid the "tourist tax" because of my "Brazilian" accent, one responded, "Well of course, professor, look at your white skin. You should have taken a Black person with you." I finally had reached full assimilation; I was a white man, but only in Africa.

Perhaps, then, it is important to ask the race question simply because it is unclear and we can participate in the joy of finding things out. Perhaps it is equally important because we have the opportunity to dismantle an academic and ecclesial house of cards that has stood for four hundred years. In either case, it is worth the effort to find out about race and how it came to play a role in the physical and human sciences and especially in theology.

It is unhistorical to perceive the concept of race before the appearance of physical anthropology proper, because the human body, as portrayed up to the time of the Renaissance and the Reformation, could not be detached from the *polis* and the *ecclesia*. Membership in both was inextricably bound to political theory and Christian Theology, and both implied a specific form of citizenship and civil order that derived its practical and moral values from the thought of the ancient world, Augustine's *De civitate Dei* and the scholastics of the middle ages rather than from natural history and biological science.[3]

Race as a Scientific Construct

It is a sad state of affairs, but when we speak of races among humans, we are speaking of biological fantasies. Race as a biological datum never existed; it has as little scientific value as the medieval alchemist's calculations in his attempts to turn lead into gold. Physical and biological anthropologists have abandoned it as a meaningful category. Geneticists and molecular biologists have long declared the idea of distinct human races a moribund concept. Health care professionals continue to maintain statistics, but as they compare their figures concerning morbidity and race with morbidity and income or morbidity and the nature of available health care, preventive intervention, diet, and lifestyle, they are increasingly convinced that these differences, which had once been perceived as racial, are, in fact, reflections of the combination of these other *sociological* factors. Already in 1952, Claude Lévi-Strauss pointed out that race was an anthropological construct rather than a biological reality. He began to dismantle the idea of a linear progression of social and technological developments across all cultures.[4]

Most of us grew up under the impression that there are three (Caucasian, Asiatic, African) or perhaps five (adding Malay and American Indian) races among human beings.[5] This idea is most often accepted as a fact. Why is this so? What was the evidence for these theories of races? Of course the liberation theologian's ever-present tool of deconstruction—the question "Whose interest is served?"—must be addressed.

The Emergence of Race as a Formal Category

This concept of race has not always been with us. It is not an idea that comes down through all of Western civilization. In fact, depending on whom one trusts, this modern concept of race and the attendant racialization of societies are phenomena that are at most four hundred years old. This pair, the concept and the attendant formalization of a competitive progressive model of the development of the races, grew up in the same era as the development of the "science" of anthropology and the nearly simultaneous application of these anthropological models to the study of the Hebrew Scriptures, the Old

Testament. Such a connection makes this history an important topic for the modern Bible scholar and one more justification for the study of race in biblical studies. This is most obvious in the likelihood that it was through religious institutions, not the universities, that popular notions of race were disseminated.[6] Further, when they were preached from the pulpits to the populace, they were presented not as scientific theories that would be repeatedly tested against new evidence, but as religious truths linked to the concepts of natural law and divine ordering of the universe.

The Harvard University solution is to blame it on the Germans. In May 2001 they sponsored an international congress with the title "The German Invention of Race."[7] The theory behind this conference is that late in the Enlightenment the confluence of several fields of study—ancient history, linguistics, religion, and the creation of the new discipline of anthropology, which is usually credited to Johann Friedrich Blumenbach—led to the invention of the modern concept of races. It seems wise to wait for the publication of the Harvard congress in book form. In the meantime one can listen to other voices of those who would make the Germans only co-conspirators with the English and the French, who, sometimes unwittingly and sometimes with malicious intent, worked to establish a European dominance over all of humankind.[8]

The Spanish were not passive viewers of this drama of Atlantic racialization. While one may wish to find a simple solution in the Harvard conference's title and some of the solutions offered by the scholarship offered there, and while Blumenbach is the acknowledged father of the modern secular concept of race, María Elena Martínez's evidence forces one to look deeper.[9] It makes clear first that the processes that gave us the phenomenon of Atlantic racism, or racialization, are quite complex and tangled, and second that Hannaford's distinction between religious racism and secular racism is quite important.[10]

Martínez traces the concept of "pure blood" *(limpieza de sangre)* from the deliberations of the high council of the Spanish Inquisition *(la Suprema)* beginning in the fifteenth century, when it was developed to prevent "new Christians,"

the direct descendents of recently con-
verted Jews and Muslims, from entry into
the highest or most sensitive areas of Spanish Christian society and government.[11]

The pure-blood standard was later ap-
plied in the New World to address the
questions of identifying indigenous peoples and African slaves in the Americas,
the children of Spaniards *(criollos)*, and
the children of a union between a
Spaniard and an indigenous person or
African *(mestizos)*. Martínez indicates the
sociopolitical marks of each of these issues and mentions in passing the completely spurious applications of the
rulings against people who were clearly
Spanish Christians and the even more
spurious practices reinterpreting the Inquisition's idolatry statutes and applying
them to cases in which the precedent of *la
Suprema* had already declared that the
laws of *limpieza de sangre* could not
apply to most indigenous peoples and
some Africans, since they were heathens
and not pagans.[12] These laws were developed to prevent Jews and Muslims from
falling back to their (or their forebears')
previous religions; since Africans and indigenous Americans had no religions,
they could not relapse.

In a sense, Martínez's research illustrates how religious terms—developed in Spain in response to the conversion of Jews and Muslims—were transferred to biological and regional situations in New-World Spanish colonies. Hannaford describes this process as the secularization of a religious idea of belonging to a distinct people. In both New Spain and Germany the classification of the Jews (and Muslims according to Martínez's research) was linked with the classification of Africans. The rationales were different: the New Spain conquistadors tried and failed to impose the classification developed for New Christians upon the African slaves, then fell back on the argument that, since their baptisms were forced and collective and rather pro forma, they had never voluntarily accepted the authority of Christ and his earthly vicar, the Holy See.

In his book *Black Athena,* Martin Bernal sets out to convince the reader that modern interpreters of the ancient world are in a rut that formed in the late Enlightenment.[13] For Bernal this path has become so fixed that we can barely imagine traveling in another direction. This fixed vision makes it impossible to see new landscapes or make new decisions about who our cultural ancestors were, and therefore who we are and might become. Bernal argues that we ignore the Greeks themselves and the very evidence that they left behind so that we can make them into who we need them to be to support our Western prejudices.

Hannaford's critical look at the West in his book *Race* is an attempt to understand where the idea of race came from. He contends that most of our modern notions of race are based on a concept that the ancient Greeks or Romans would not have recognized. He also believes that during the Enlightenment, Western interpreters distorted the concept of "citizen" found in Plato's *Republic* and *Timeus*. He argues that a need to justify the establishment of a hierarchy of civilizations led to the creation of the idea of race. The sources he cites crisscross and intertwine with those cited by Bernal in interesting and sometimes contradictory ways. But they are in general agreement that, during the Enlightenment, old religious hatreds, tribal rivalries, and cultural clashes combined with contemporary fears, the developing modern sciences, and the emergence of the European nation-states.

These forces, coupled with a sense of relief and pride after the expulsion of the Jews and Muslims from Spain and a new awareness of the enormous breadth of the earth and its peoples, imposed upon us a racialized New World, most of it connected by the Atlantic.

Blumenbach's *De Generis Humani Varietate Natura* was published in its first edition in 1775. Hannaford and Bernal alike are careful to point out that in this first edition, the word *varietas* is used to describe the "marvelous diversity of humankind," but by the third edition twenty years later *gens* and *genitilltius* have supplanted the term throughout the work.[14] They also stress that he was a *monogenesist,* preferring to maintain a connection to the biblical story of the creation of all humankind from one source; he would also support its accompanying theory that humanity was preserved in Genesis 6–9 and that the most perfect of all original humanity, Noah and his offspring, were deposited in the Caucasus mountains to repopulate the earth. Initially, both scientific observations and *a priori* preclusions lead Blumenbach to insist on one race, human.

Hannaford also makes it clear that Blumenbach rejected the most absurd claim (and perhaps most common) of his day that suggested a separation of humans and attempted to place one race closer to the "animal kingdom" than another. Of course, those who wished to do this would have placed the "Caucasian race" as the most highly developed, and, of course, Blumenbach described the Caucasian human as the most beautiful. It was the basic or normal human from which all others degenerated. This degeneration of humanity was brought about by external differences such as climate and diet.[15]

Hannaford presents a sympathetic Blumenbach who argued against the rush of his colleagues to place the African in a semi-human or nonhuman species between the beautiful Caucasian and the apes. Since at that time the major arguments for the classification of humans were based on a seventeenth-century interpretation of the Greek standards of beauty, Blumenbach countered that if one were serious about the classification, some Europeans were not really human either. Observation would reveal as many ugly

Europeans as Africans.[16] Unfortunately, it seems that the pressure to distinguish Caucasians from their darker siblings was too great for Blumenbach to resist. By 1780 he had exhausted the possibilities available to him via observation to explain the visible differences in humans.

Bernal's evaluation of Blumenbach is nearly as positive as Hannaford's.[17] This is an indication that the culprit is not the nascent field of anthropology itself, but as is usually the case, the use of anthropology in the service of "god and country." Finally, Hannaford sums up Blumenbach's contribution in the following:

Despite Blumenbach's evidence that . . . man and beast were distinct and that there was no physical relationship between the Negro and the orang-utan, there remained lingering doubts about the subtle divisions within his exploratory classifications system. During the last forty years of his long life controversy raged over items he had put squarely on the agenda: de-generation, the formative force, the significance of language and milieu (geography, climate, relief, soil, land),

and, perhaps most important of all, the capacity of peoples for progressive physical, moral, and political development.[18]

Jonathan Hess's work on the German language and literature of the romantic period suggests that Blumenbach's colleague, J. D. Michaelis of Göttingen—the man normally credited with introducing anthropological methods to the study of the Old Testament—was instrumental in the racialization of anthropology.[19] Ironically, but understandably, Michaelis's contribution took shape in the midst of discussions about the emancipation of the Jews: During the Enlightenment Jewish and African destinies were placed on parallel tracks en route to a totally racialized West. Hess argues that at the end of the Enlightenment anti-Semitism changed radically from religious bigotry to secular and "scientific" hatred. Hannaford argues that the new theories of race emergent at the end of the eighteenth century and evident in the final edition of Blumenbach's *Generis Humani Varietate Natura* radically change the perception of what it means to be human. Before the invention of physical anthropology, the Western idea of what it meant to be human was tied either to one's membership in the Christian community (the church) or one's citizenship (a status limited to the highborn). After the anthropological imposition of racial divisions within humanity, a change occurred. From this point on, one's humanity was based on a presumed set of biological "facts" and observable physical characteristics that were perceived as being normative, and indeed desirable, in Europe but degenerate in all other parts of the world, especially in southern climates.

How Do Scientists Classify Races Today?

First of all, it is important to make one thing very clear about how physical scientists divide humans into racial categories today. They do not! Below are excerpts from two position statements. The first is from the "Statement on Biological Aspects of Race" from the American Association of Physical Anthropologists (AAPA). The AAPA is comprised of professional researchers and their doctoral students who, insofar as it is possible, concentrate their research on the physiological aspects of human communities.

We offer the following points as revisions of the 1964 UNESCO statement on race:

1. All humans living today belong to a single species, *homo sapiens,* and share a common descent. Although there are differences of opinion regarding how and where the different human groups diverged or fused to form new ones from a common ancestral group, all living populations in each of the earth's geographic areas have evolved from that ancestral group over the same amount of time. Much of the biological variation among populations involves modest degrees of variation in the frequency of shared traits. Human populations have never genetically diverged enough to produce any biological barriers to mating between members of different populations. . . .

3. There is a great genetic diversity within all human populations. Pure races, in the sense of genetically homogenous populations, do not exist

in the human species today, nor is there any evidence that they ever existed in the past.[20]

The second excerpted statement is from the American Anthropological Association, the largest scientific society of anthropologists in the world, and addresses "Race and Intelligence." Adopted in December 1994, it was written in part as a response to *The Bell Curve,* the pseudo-scientific book published in 1994 that proposed to explain some profound differences in academic performance between "racial" groups.[21] In so doing, the authors fall back on an essentialist eighteenth- and nineteenth-century argument of a mysterious genetic inferiority in African and African American persons.

> All human beings are members of one species, *Homo sapiens.* . . . Differentiating species into biologically defined "races" has proven meaningless and unscientific as a way of explaining variation (whether in intelligence or other traits).[22]

At the beginning of the West's third millennium, race is not a tool that the physical sciences take seriously. It is a meaningful tool only for *social* scientists. The next chapter will treat the anthropological aspects of race in an effort to prepare the reader for a discussion of (1) race's role in Western religion since race was invented, (2) how modern societies constructed themselves on the basis of racial and other social categories, (3) how race has become a real, if not legitimate, category for theological reflections, (4) how what moderns call "race" might have been viewed in the ancient world, and finally, (5) a discussion of how all of this affects the way we think about our history in the West and how we understand ourselves as human beings and as people of faith.

2
Race and Religion

Since I first began studying theology there has been a proliferation of "theologies" in the universities, colleges, and divinity schools of the Americas. This proliferation is due, in part, to the recognition that all theology is contextual and linked to the experiences of those engaged in theological production. These varied experiences cannot be separated from the physical realities that we live without distorting the theology or damaging the soul of the theologian or both. These theologies—which acknowledge, rather than obscure or ignore, their contexts and their incarnational bases—have generally been called "liberation theologies."

At the beginning of the 1960s there was no published Black theology, no feminist theology, no Latin American liberation theology, and no Asian theologies published. Certainly there was no gay or womanist theology in print. There were, of course, theologies or theological treatments by women and by Blacks. Without a doubt gay men and lesbians have been writing Christian theology since the inception of the church, but they did not identify their theological points of departure as their experiences of body and mind. The old ecclesiastical worldview for the most part ignored women. It is exactly because it was feared that women's bodies would contaminate their minds' productions that many women too refrained from naming their integrated human—and therefore corporeal—experiences as theological tools.

Some of the theologies mentioned above, especially feminist theologies, have made their way into the curricula of European and American universities. In Africa, some note has been taken of North America's Black theologies, whose beginnings can be marked by the publication of James Cone's *Black Theology and Black Power* in 1969.[1] Theologians in Africa began producing theologies based in the struggles for independence; most notable among these are the works of Zimbabwean and South African Black leaders. In the 1990s the conversations among Africans, South Americans, and

Asians began making their way into the "general" theological conversation.

These "movement" theologies or "contextual" theologies, as some have chosen to call them, are in some cases attempts to add some texture to the theological conversations taking place in the academic world. In other cases they represent a blatant rejection of the way theology was being done in the second half of the twentieth century. People of color and some European and Euro-American women decided that since they found themselves systematically excluded from the academic discussion that understands itself as the mainstream of theology, they would ignore that discussion to varying degrees. In some cases they spoke only to their identified constituency, and thus conversation with the academic models of theological study became superfluous. It was not a matter of "winning over" the major thinkers of the respective theological fields to one position or another of one of the new theologies, nor was it even a matter of gaining space in the mainstream academy for these differently oriented theologies; though it must be said that this certainly happened. By the beginning of the 1990s, most of these theologies had chairs or at least professors at major theological centers. Even the most risky of the theologies, gay and lesbian theologies, had strongholds in distinguished institutions on each coast of the United States.

African American biblical scholars, who grew up with Cone's early texts, usually as supplemental readings in their theological education, rejected the basic racialized premises of theology as it was being done in the United States, but they continued to study the methodology and acquire the tools of the flagging historical-critical schools. Living in two worlds, the university and the Black church tradition, they live without contradiction. A model of that dual tradition was that of the Rev. Dr. Martin Luther King Jr.—churchman, scholar, statesman, and activist. Like many black religious scholars of their day, these men and women refused to see the academy and their religious lives as divergent paths. They refused to believe that one must choose between "knowing" one's religious heritage and living it.

All of this was part of a general and decided de-centering of theological thinking and theological production in the Americas and to some extent in Africa. No longer did we look to Europe for all forms of enlightenment. We began to believe that truth also could be found in the libraries and classrooms and in the streets and homes of the lands on the western shores of the Atlantic Ocean—not that *the* truth could be found, but truths, each community's, each individual's part of the greater truths of human existence and celebration in the presence of God.

We are not amused when we hear from some European and Euro-American colleagues that we are not engaged in real "scientific" inquiry but in some social science of ambiguous definition. Nor are we pleased when we find books and articles relegated to the shelves of practical theology or contextual theology. This is a general issue for American theological researchers, but it is acute among researchers of color. This irritation is especially acute in the case of any theology that grows from human experiences and can be perceived as a social issue. It is a farcical maintenance of the untenable separation of body and soul. It is a pretentious illusion that there is something pure and objective about the way theology has been done in the Western church, as if it were handed down directly by the Almighty to the theologians of the correct methodology. Somehow, the great fathers of theology from the first century to the middle of the twentieth century are presented as having practiced their craft without any social context, and then suddenly, Asians, women, Blacks, gays, and Latin Americans began infecting the theological purity with their bodies and their body-oriented questions and assertions.

Any theological inquiry that has a specific human experience as its point of departure is considered suspect. It seems that we would rather speculate with Immanuel Kant and his *Critique of Pure Reason* (the work of a man who never ventured a hundred miles from his own home) than trust in the experience of people with a slightly broader experience—men and women who have gone about in the world and understand that their set of experiences are but one among many.

When I write of a "European" way of thinking about theology, I mean a way of thinking based in theory rather than experience—reason on its own terms, not clouded by the emotional ties of personal relationships and experiences. This way of thinking assumes that there is something that is true for everyone at every moment and in every place one can imagine or even beyond what one can imagine. There is a center of theological reality that cannot be challenged. There is *A Truth*.

To speak of one European way of thinking theologically is, of course, a stereotype, but stereotypes often have their origins in some form of reality. Few of us on the western side of the Atlantic have read the works of all European theologians, but those whose work is widely disseminated in the Americas believe in and teach about a disembodied absolute or universal truth independent of daily experiences. Postcolonial theologies generally oppose this rejection of human theological data.

There is no disembodied logic. There is no platonic ideal; Aristotle was closer to the mark than was his teacher. George Lakoff and Mark Johnson indicate that everything we know, we know on the basis of our corporeal experiences.[2] We cannot imagine anything that is not, in some way, relatable to our embodied existence. If there is a disembodied independent and universal truth out there somewhere, we as human beings have absolutely no way of accessing it. If it does not enter through one of the five senses, it has no way to get into our imaginations. In short, we can only know what we know via metaphors. The metaphors can be extremely sophisticated and complex, but in the end, we can only extrapolate them from our sensory experiences.

3
Race and the Bible

A World of Choices
for Reading the Old Testament

Each interpreter of ancient texts makes many unacknowledged choices when he or she first approaches the text. Some of these choices are so automatic that they hardly seem choices at all. In the same way that in the so-called Christian West "race" became an unconscious choice in our organization of the world, we make assumptions about what the biblical texts are. A good example is the debate that is championed by Brevard Childs when he calls for a canonical reading of the Hebrew Scriptures. The books Genesis through Malachi comprise the Christian Old Testament, not the Hebrew or Jewish Scriptures. Surely, he is correct, in part. The ancient Western church's decisions to read the Greek and Latin versions of the

Old Testament, rather than the Hebrew and Aramaic, sent us in a particular interpretive direction. The Renaissance humanists' decision to rescue the Hebrew text for the church's use altered that direction. The modern churches' ever more frequent decision to diminish the depth of Hebrew language instruction and its attendant cultural milieu to its theological aspirants alters again the church's trajectory.

Childs's decision to understand the thirty-nine books as properly ordered with Genesis beginning the story, the book of Ruth inserted between Judges and Samuel (and the decision to read Samuel as two books rather than one), the affirmation that Chronicles should follow Kings, that Ezra and Nehemiah should come next, in turn followed by the poetic books instead of the prophets, is a choice made in the past and also by subsequent readers. Except in the tender years of confirmation instruction, this order is not forced upon us. This is a choice that the church has made—and reaffirmed many times. It makes a statement about the way that Jews and Christians differ in their interpretations of the Bible or Tanakh and the Old Testament.[1] In short, the interpreter's traditions make some choices for him or her. From there, the interpreter must decide to stand within the tradition quietly or to move about within the tradition proposing changes in its worldview.

More Conscious Choices

Other choices are more easily seen as proactive. One school of thought or another convinces the interpreter. An interpreter understands a passage in a prophetic text to be poetry rather than prose and applies the appropriate tools of interpretation to that passage as dictated by whether the text is perceived as containing antithetical or synonymous parallelism. One makes comparisons with particular texts within the prophetic canon based on one's dating of the text under consideration and its presumed *Sitz im Leben* (situation in life). When one fails to understand a practice or custom (or better, when one *realizes* that such a failure has occurred), one seeks parallels in other cultures.[2] Selecting valid sets of data is problematic.

The issues one takes up and the assumptions one makes regarding the cultures of the Old Testament and the culture of the "central family" narrative of the Old Testament, which presents Israel as an extended family, will determine in large part how one reads the text. It is important to be conscious of one's biases rather than to hide them or pretend that they do not exist. If one assumes that the Old Testament is linked to the Christian West in a more or less linear fashion, one will find connections and read the evidence to support such a vision of the Old Testament world. If, on the other hand, one believes that the Old Testament world is connected to the Christian West in a decidedly less direct fashion, one sees the evidence differently.

Choices That Have Been Blocked

Since the Enlightenment, beginning with the highly esteemed Göttingen school of Old Testament studies and its accompanying development of Orientalism, the Western university has assumed itself to be the best seat of interpretation of ancient Hebraic texts and the customs they relate. It has presumed itself to be unfettered by the prejudices and superstitions of religious believers, be they Jewish or

Christian. It is nearly self-evident, however, that the predominant faith of the scholars who have held these distinguished chairs of Semitic philology, Hebrew Scripture, and Old Testament and those who hold them yet today has overwhelmingly been a sort of Christianized academic civil religion that supports the foundational principles of the Christian West.

Researchers have usurped the position of arbiter of "God's Word," and, like the Renaissance painters and sculptors, we have refashioned both the inhabitants of those texts and their meaning in our own image. When Michaelis sent the famous ill-fated 1761 Danish expedition off to Egypt and what is today Yemen with its list of questions to be researched, he did so with the understanding that Jews were not competent to interpret Israelite and Judahite History. When the expedition abandoned Egypt and its southern and southeastern neighbors, the group ignored the millennial connections among Egyptians, Cushites/Ethiopians, and Nubians in favor of the region now known as Yemen, a choice that would guide Old Testament research away from Africa for centuries. From this point forward, Egypt's connections with Africa, modern Ethiopia, and the Sudan were denied; the process of de-Africanizing Egypt had begun. Perhaps the belief that the supposedly superior culture of Egypt could not have suffered true parity with Africans (many researchers well into the second half of the twentieth century insisted that the Egyptians were phenotypically Caucasoid rather than Negroid!), much less have African roots, led Michaelis to opt for Yemen rather than its ancient suzerain, Ethiopia, as a possible source for anthropological data. It is clear that Michaelis chose Egypt as a starting point in part because he believed it would reveal Caucasian rather than Semitic roots of the Decalogue, the Western religious masterpiece. He believed Semites incapable of such moral-ethical elevation.[3]

This decision to go to the Bedouin of the Arabian Peninsula rather than to the area where the Egyptians lived and incubated their culture is peculiar, but it makes sense when one sees that Michaelis understood the Egyptian culture to be an insertion rather than an extension of African culture. Its effect was to cut off the possibility that universities would look to Africa as a legitimate source of information as to who were our religious forebears.

Niels Peter Lemche is among the growing number of formerly traditional Old Testament exegetes who have stepped back from the trees in an attempt to see the forest.[4] He questions the dominant method of reading the ancient texts of the Western faiths and challenges our assumptions about the texts' worldview. He suggests that we might learn more from African contexts and African interpreters, whose worldview has more in common with that of the ancients than the typical Western exegete's worldview does.

When we read Hebrew Scriptures with our contemporary categories, we do damage to them and impede our ability to understand them. He cites examples of how we look for logical explanations in the metaphors and where we fail to see the supernatural that was part of the *Sitz im Leben* of the text, and coincidentally many African cultures. Later I will argue that Lemche has stopped short. Our university training (note the use of the word *training* rather than *education* at this point) has impeded and often even prohibited us from seeing the possibility that these two sets of worldviews, the African and the Old Testament, are directly connected.

In the South African *Journal of North-west Semitic Languages* one can read the criticism of C. H. J. van der Merwe's long running challenge to the Western method of teaching about the ancient Israelite and Judahite cultures via the Hebrew language. [5] Beginning in the early 1980s he has written about the history of exegesis from the perspective of Indo-European linguistic categories and assumptions. He begins the conclusion to his 1996 essay with these words:

> It appears that in the very good old days, Jewish scholars knew a relatively great deal about the grammar of BH [Biblical Hebrew] as well how it was used to communicate in the OT [Old Testament]. Divorcing the study and teaching of BH grammar from rhetoric and concentrating on the forms of the language has, unfortunately, resulted in a very reduced picture of what constitutes knowledge of BH.[6]

Lemche and van der Merwe, working on the edges of the Western academy,

Copenhagen and Stellenbosch, illustrate both how the academy can be self-critical and how it has failed to take advantage of all the possible tools for interpreting ancient texts. Lemche suggests that traditional worldviews[7] are necessary for understanding traditional collections of texts. Van der Merwe, while advocating a more global approach to the teaching of Hebrew for biblical scholars, implies that the Christian West erred when it took the Hebrew Bible from the hands of the Jews and declared them incompetent interpreters of their own tradition.

In what follows, I will outline another possibility for reading the texts of the Hebrew Bible—one that has been developing for at least four hundred years, has slowly entered the academy in the United States over the past fifty years, and has enjoyed a critical mass of academic scholars only in the past twenty years.[8] I suggest reading the Hebrew Bible while staying open to the possibility, or even having the conviction, that it makes as much sense to look to Africa as to Asia Minor and Mesopotamia for hints as to what the texts meant in their contexts. Indeed, this new reading would see many of the characters in the Hebrew Bible as Africans or Afro-descendents.

This, however, is only a first step. It is time to acknowledge that the choices Michaelis made in the second half of the eighteenth century were in part based on his racism toward Africans and his assumption that they were incapable of establishing a highly organized society with a fully developed intellectual life. In addition to his prejudices, Michaelis was hindered by a lack of information. He had a very limited exposure to African cultures, and many of the things we know about African societies were not available to researchers of the seventeenth century. The elaborate ruins of the medieval African society of Great Zimbabwe (from which the modern state takes its name), for example, remained unknown to Europeans until the nineteenth century.

Recent developments in genetics, linguistics, and anthropology encourage researchers to look to different geographical regions:

Archaeology: The Oriental Institute's excavations at Qutsul have demonstrated that the Nubians in the royal tombs can reasonably be described as protopharaonic.[9]

Genetic Information: The reader has already seen that the nature of physical anthropological or biological data and its evaluation have changed. Very few biologists, geneticists, or biological anthropologists involved in serious research hold and teach theories of genetic hierarchies.

Linguistics: The recognition of the Afroasiatic family of languages and the fact that they have similarities and connections that stretch from Mesopotamia to the foot of Mount Kilimanjaro now make it possible to establish linguistic connections not only with the peoples of northern Africa but also with some of the Bantu people in deep sub-Saharan Africa.[10]

Literary Studies: 1. Scholars have established, especially in wisdom literature, parallel structure and suggested parallel functions between the respective societies.[11]

2. Better known are Westermann's suggestions that one read some narratives in primeval history in light of African stories.[12] These readings may come under the category of cultural connections, although the connection is yet to be established. There is no doubt that these data can be used in the category of cultural anthropological data.

3. Finally, there is the changing face of the field of biblical studies. When Michaelis wrote, there was one African theologian at the University of Halle. Since 1967, nearly ninety Africans have earned doctorates in Old Testament.[13]

New Possibilities

If one is open to the possibility that the peoples who populated the Old Testament were people of color, or Black to be more specific, one has a variety of options to support this possibility. Charles Copher spent a good deal of his publishing energy as Professor of Old Testament at the Interdenominational Theological Center writing about the Black presence in the Bible. He systematized what was already known in African American church circles and probed deeper into the history of the ancient Near East with an eye toward seeing if it were possible to read Africa back into the texts of the Old Testament. He researched in the face of the Anglo-American and German hegemonies over the fields of research of the Hebrew Bible and attendant fields such as philology and archaeology.[14]

In what follows I will outline four ways to think about the African roots of the Old Testament peoples. One can think of the first three ways of applying the modern racialized concept of peoples and their colors—which continues to develop in the United States—as attempts to understand people of African descent as agents in their own histories. This includes, of course, their religious histories.

Reading via Genealogy

The easiest way to illustrate an African cast to the people of Israel are the genealogical statements that a certain person is the descendent of a person designated by a term indicating Egyptian, Cushitic, Nubian, or Libyan origins. The following are examples that have been treated with varying degrees of acceptance in the academy. The first is Zephaniah the prophet:

> The word of the LORD that came to Zephaniah son of Cushi son of Gedaliah son of Amariah son of Hezekiah, in the days of King Josiah son of Amon of Judah. (Zeph 1:1)

The second is the Cushite messenger who brings news of Absalom's death to King David:

> Then the Cushite came; and the Cushite said, "Good tidings for my lord the king! For the LORD has vindicated you this day, delivering you from the power of all who rose up against you." The king said to the Cushite, "Is it well with the young man Absalom?" The Cushite answered, "May the enemies of my lord the king, and all who rise up to do you harm, be like that young man." (2 Sam 18:31-32)

A third example is Zerah, the mighty general defeated at Gerar:

> Zerah the Ethiopian came out against them with an army of a million men and three hundred chariots, and came as far as Mareshah. Asa went out to meet him, and they drew up their lines of battle in the valley of Zephathah at Mareshah. Asa cried to the LORD his God, "O LORD, there is no difference for you between helping the mighty and the weak. Help us, O LORD our God, for we rely on you, and

in your name we have come against this multitude. O LORD, you are our God; let no mortal prevail against you." So the LORD defeated the Ethiopians before Asa and before Judah, and the Ethiopians fled. Asa and the army with him pursued them as far as Gerar, and the Ethiopians fell until no one remained alive; for they were broken before the LORD and his army. The people of Judah carried away a great quantity of booty. They defeated all the cities around Gerar, for the fear of the LORD was on them. (2 Chron 14:9-14)

Yet another example is Ishmael, the father of all Arabs (according to tradition) and the son of Hagar, Abraham's second wife, who was Egyptian:

So, after Abram had lived ten years in the land of Canaan, Sarai, Abram's wife, took Hagar the Egyptian, her slave-girl, and gave her to her husband Abram as a wife. He went in to Hagar, and she conceived. . . . The angel of the LORD said to her,
        "Now you have conceived and
            shall bear a son;

> you shall call him Ishmael,
> for the LORD has given heed
>   to your affliction. . . ."
> (Gen 16:3-4, 11)

There are also Ishmael's descendents:

> God was with the boy, and he grew
> up; he lived in the wilderness, and be-
> came an expert with the bow. He lived
> in the wilderness of Paran; and his
> mother got a wife for him from the
> land of Egypt. (Gen 21:20-21)

In addition, there is Jehudi, the messenger sent to Baruch to fetch Jeremiah's
scroll:

> And Micaiah told them all the words
> that he had heard, when Baruch read
> the scroll in the hearing of the people.
> Then all the officials sent Jehudi son
> of Nethaniah son of Shelemiah son of
> Cushi to say to Baruch, "Bring the
> scroll that you read in the hearing of
> the people, and come." So Baruch son
> of Neriah took the scroll in his hand
> and came to them. (Jer 36:13-14)

And another example is Gershom, one of
the family heads who returned from the

Babylonian Exile to Jerusalem with Ezra; he is of African descent through Phinehas:

> These are their family heads, and this is the genealogy of those who went up with me from Babylonia, in the reign of King Artaxerxes: Of the descendants of Phinehas,[15] Gershom. Of Ithamar, Daniel. Of David, Hattush, of the descendants of Shecaniah. Of Parosh, Zechariah, with whom were registered one hundred fifty males. (Ezra 8:1-3)

Reading via Geography

The fact that the peoples who live the "holy histories" of Israel and Judah are in constant contact with Africa—especially, but not limited to, Egypt—is an important indication that there was a fair amount of cultural interchange, usually with high culture flowing from Egypt to southern Palestine.[16]

Early in the narrative of Gen 12:10-20, Abram and Sarai descend to Egypt in danger of starvation and exit well fed and wealthy. The outline of this story is repeated twice, once in Genesis 20 and again in Genesis 26. In these second and third occurrences, Gerar is named as the locale and Sarah and Abraham and Isaac and Rebecca are the protagonists. The sons of Israel descended with their father and live for four hundred years in Africa.[17] At some point in this extended visit, the families grow to such a size that they become a threat to the throne of Egypt and are enslaved. Finally, they exit from the land, but not before at least two celebrated marriages to women of the region. Joseph marries the daughter of an influential priest, and throughout the four hundred years, according to the story, the two sons of this marriage take their places as half-tribes of the people of Israel. Moses, at some point near the end of this period of what had become slavery, married an Ethiopian woman. It is unclear if this woman is the same Zipporah of Exodus 3 or a different wife. There is a fair amount of confusion about this matter, and it seems that there is no easy solution since the evidence concerning Midian (Zipporah and her family are identified as Midianites) and its relation to Ethiopia in the middle of the second half of the second millennium B.C.E. is obscure. Nevertheless, Maricel Mena López has presented evidence that Ethiopia was the suzerain on both shores of the Red Sea during this period. Mena understands Zipporah and the Ethiopian to be one and the same.[18]

Each of these narratives has its own weight to lend to an overall Afro-Israelite worldview. What is more significant, however, is the basic datum of a tradition of four hundred years as residents in the land of Egypt with all of the attendant contact with her neighbors. It seems logical that a people living four hundred years in a defined space come to think of themselves as part of the landscape and that very landscape then begins to affect the persons interacting in it.

It is significant, for example, that even the narratives of the escape from bondage—the Exodus traditions—acknowledge the deep connections that the Hebrews have with their former neighbors and their homeland. While they are often interpreted as moments of indecisiveness or of adolescence or courtship between Yahweh and the people/nation in formation, it is also possible to read the moments in the wilderness when the Hebrews longed to return to the familiar toils of their former Egyptian homelands as hints of *saudade* (a longing for the emotional and physical comforts and securities of one's home) for their birthplaces and the very homes in which they birthed and reared their children.[19] One witness even indicates that the Egyptians (dare one say, as opposed to the Egyptian nobility?) were kindly disposed toward the Hebrews even as they departed with their gold jewelry.

> The Israelites had done as Moses told them; they had asked the Egyptians for jewelry of silver and gold, and for clothing, and the LORD had given the people favor in the sight of the Egyptians, so that they let them have what they asked. And so they plundered the Egyptians. (Exod 12:35-36)

The prophetic traditions also repeat the need to leave behind or not to return to the dependency upon Egypt as source of security. Here again, this dependency on the foreign king is considered an affront to Yahweh's sovereignty, a demonstration of a lack of confidence in the "true" salvation. Finally, the Psalms and the various historiographies recount the passage in Egypt as formative moments in the lives of the Hebrews/Israelites.

Proverbs 22:17–24:34, with its obvious dependence on the Instructions of Amenemope, represents a clear connection between the Egyptian wisdom tradition and its cousins in the Israelite tradition. There can be little doubt now that the citations in the book of Proverbs are a reflection of Palestinians suffering Egyptian cultural dominance.

The preceding are all examples of a collection of memories that recall Africa as the literal and cultural breeding ground of the Israelite identity at its inception. The following narratives point out the close ties with Egypt during the cultural high point of the united monarchy (the reign of Solomon as opposed to the glory days of David) and the period immediately before the Babylonian Exile, when Judah quite naturally sought refuge from her older sister to the south.

Reading via Anthropology

Here I would include two subcategories or methods: (1) reading from parallel practices and (2) reading from myths of origins and key narratives that form identity. I begin with the second subcategory.

The stories of the origins of the Israelites can be useful for understanding how they understood themselves and the world around them. This is not to suggest that we take the stories literally, but literarily. These stories are useful because they can provide anthropological data without being taken as anthropological statements. That they are somewhat indicative of the cosmology of their day has been debated, accepted, redebated, and refined since the days of Julius Wellhausen. While few would argue that these stories of the creation of the earth and all it contains were understood as historical treatments that jibe with our modern way of understanding history, today very few would argue that the stories do not give us at least a minimum of historical data. In much the same fashion that they provide us some historical data without being taken as history, they offer data about perceptions that we would classify today as social-scientific. I think it is beyond dispute, for example, that Judah's emotional bonds with Egypt were much more complex than the exodus and prophetic traditions would initially lead one to believe.

Many have argued that we can glean an idea of how the ancients thought or did not think about the sociological phenomenon that moderns call race from these texts.[20] I accept the premise without accepting all of the cases they have presented. Comments concerning one or another of the distinguishing characteristics or relative power of the neighbors, whether they were friends or foes, or concerning their appearances can be interpreted in a positive manner. This attitude is quite different from the general tone assumed by key interpreters of the modern West.[21]

An example might be the second creation narrative that relates the creation of humanity from the mud or clay of the riverbank. This can be understood as one indication of how these men and women understood their forebears to have been molded in the hands of the great deity. It seems unlikely that such a story would originate among a people who did not have complexions somewhat akin to the color of the earth from which they understood themselves to have been formed. Another indication of this is the fact that they see themselves as not-so-distant cousins of the Egyptians, the Libyans, the Ethiopians, and the *Canaanites.*

At the end of the story of the universal flood in Genesis 9 and in the Table of Nations in Genesis 10, we read about the repopulation of the entire Earth from the seed of Noah's sons and their wives, the other survivors of the great deluge. This myth assumes a great connection among all humankind. It was one of the little-spoken justifications for the division of the world into three great "races" by early anthropologists in the eighteenth century. Shem was thought to represent the Asiatic types, Ham the African types, and Jafe the European types. It is worth noting that Jafe, the European line of the family of Noah, is almost completely absent from the other stories of the Israelites and Judahites. The offspring of Shem and Ham were in near constant contact in the narratives of origins.

Also important, these stories show that, while there may have been an observation of phenotypic characteristics among peoples, there was not a sense that they were so distant as to be unrecognizable as fellow human beings who were born from the same mythological or eponymous ancestor. The greater differences of the sons of Jafe could nevertheless be explained by their long absence from the territory of their ultimate origins.

The material cultures of the Israelites and their Hamitic cousins and rivals the Canaanites are almost indistinguishable. The sociological arguments for the theory that peasant revolt rather than an exodus from Egypt made for the beginnings of Israel even use these similarities to suggest that at times they are one and the same culture. Ironically, the same evidence so often used to support a "racially pure" Israel can be read to support an Afro-Asiatic Israel.

If one reads Genesis 38 with an eye critical of the assumption that characters are pre-Europeans rather than extended Africans, one sees in the story that Judah, perhaps horrified by his complicity in the sale of his own brother into slavery in Egypt, departs the company of his remaining brothers and goes down alone into Canaanite territory. If the Judahites had been concerned with racial purity in any "modern" sense of the phrase, this story could not stand in the canon. It is interesting how it plays itself out, perhaps even against some protest by "purists." In just eleven verses, we see Judah estrange himself from his family, take a foreign wife, sire three sons, become a widower, and marry off and lose the first two sons to the same woman, a local. It is most likely that she was also a Canaanite since there is no genealogy given in the text that would connect her to the sacred family, as was the case with Isaac's marriage to Rebecca and Jacob's marriages to Leah and Rachel.

Just when it seems that the sacred line of Abraham has escaped contamination by foreign—and, I add, mythological—African blood, in the following twenty-seven verses, Tamar, the suspected Canaanite, does what so many women in the Old Testament do: she takes the initiative, acts outrageously, and preserves the sacred line. She plays the harlot, seduces her father-in-law, and becomes pregnant with the twins who will replace the two deceased sons of Judah. The sacred line is saved. The line is half-Semitic and half-Hamitic, if one reads the mythological sub-text with an eye to the African aspect of the Old Testament.

From these stories and others, one can also look for parallel practices in Afro-Asiatic cultures.[22] It remains to define just how one guards against lumping everything into one, thus avoiding giving either Israelite or individual African cultures their due particularity. Nevertheless, the Levirate marriage, a significant custom in the narratives of the line of David, has key parallels throughout modern Africa.

Reading via Theology

In his landmark work, *Black Theology and Black Power,* James Cone suggested that race was more of a sociological construct than a biological reality. For Cone, the Black person was one who suffered oppression by the dominant society; in this way, Cone was able to maintain a connection with current South and Central American social movements that were finding their own theological voices in the form of Latin American liberation theology.[23] I suspect that he was also concerned with the Asian liberation movements that had a considerably smaller proportion of Christians who would find their voices in the late 1970s and more forcefully in the 1980s.

Cone's reading of the Bible, like that of his Latin American interlocutors, had a strong footing in the Exodus stories and their attendant motifs. That God chose Israel not out of its merit but out of its need, that righteousness was imputed to Abram, and that God remained steadfastly with his family because of the haplessness of the Hebrews and not *in spite* of it, were important elements. They were important for understanding why one should believe in God in the midst of increasing suffering and poverty, while the wealth of a limited few was growing in every corner of the world. Cone and his interlocutors around the world knew that their seemingly isolated problems were not really isolated but pieces of the same socioeconomic puzzle. In Cone's view, this puzzle was not designed by an all-powerful deity who sent the slaves to the brickyard but by the pharaohs whom God would eventually drown in the Red Sea.

Cone's theological points, aligned with his social-scientific and economic points of view, allowed him to see men and women as "Black" who either suffered in their own settings the same oppression as North American Blacks in the United States or entered into solidarity with them or their parallels in other cultures. It was a reversal of fortunes to suddenly see Black as the preferred color, the color favored by God.[24]

Conclusions

It is odd to conclude an essay that begins so vehemently arguing against race as a biologically meaningful category by insisting that race matters in biblical interpretation. Nevertheless, the powers of the Atlantic world have used the category for so long that it has become necessary to employ it in order to deconstruct the myth that our modern and supposedly natural categories of race existed in the ancient world. This book attempts to point to three important changes in Old Testament studies in the past twenty years. First, it highlights the gradual realization that race is an anthropological and political category rather than a category of the natural sciences. Second, it illustrates that the exegetical field's error of accepting either of these categorizations as natural, usually with attendant assumptions of a racial hierarchy that assumes the intellectual and moral superiority of the Caucasians, has hampered our understanding of the text by unnecessarily eliminating possible avenues of study. Third, it shows clearly that Israel and Judah cannot be separated from their African roots and artificially counted as a type of proto-European people.

As more artifacts come out of the ground in the areas that were once Cush, Meroe, Nubia, and perhaps even Sheba (just across the Red Sea from Cush), we understand more and more that Egypt was not an isolated miracle on the Nile but part of a lively world of trade, intellectual exchange, romance, and warfare. In the next decades we will be able to test theories that make it necessary to speak of an Afro-Asian worldview in the way that we now speak of a Mediterranean world beginning in the Roman period and an Atlantic world in the age of discovery in the Americas.

Notes

1. Talking about Race

1. Richard P. Feynman, "The Relation of Science and Religion," in *The Pleasure of Finding Things Out* (London: Penguin, 2001), 247–48.

2. In this study *racialization* is used to designate the creation of groupings among human beings called *races* and the subsequent imputation of significance to racial categories where none exists.

3. Ivan Hannaford, *Race: The History of an Idea in the West* (Baltimore: Johns Hopkins University Press, 1996), 147.

4. Claude Lévi-Strauss, *Race and History,* The Race Question in Modern Science (Paris: UNESCO, 1952).

5. These five terms represent the groups that Johann Friedrich Blumenbach introduced to the world based on his observations of human skulls and other physical characteristics. Caucasian was used for the first time in the second edition of *De Generis Humani Varietate Natura* in 1781. He also switched from the term *Mongolian* to *Asiatic* at this point. Hannaford, *Race,* 207–8.

6. Göttingen's academic calendar from March of 1790 lists fifty-three professors, and thirty-eight other teachers who "also belonged to the academic

staff (teachers of mathematics or foreign languages) without the status of a university professor." Bärbel Mund of the Niedersächische Staats- und Universitätsbibliothek provided these figures. They are a result of her examination of Göttingigische Anzeigen von gelehrten Sachen. I am grateful to Mrs. Mund for taking up the cause of an unknown researcher from across the Atlantic and to her supervisor, Dr. Helmut Rohlfing, who allowed her to take the time on my behalf. Personal correspondence, May 3, 2002.

7. The interdisciplinary congress took place May 4–6, 2001, and was sponsored by the Afro-American Studies and German departments and the Max Kade Foundation.

8. Kathryn Tanner's book *Theories of Culture* is important for understanding the theological ramifications of these late Renaissance and early Enlightenment developments, especial her first chapter and her outline of the varying concepts of culture. See Kathryn Tanner, *Theories of Culture: A New Agenda for Theology,* Guides to Theological Inquiry (Minneapolis: Fortress Press, 1997).

9. María Elena Martínez, "Religion, Purity, and Race: The Spanish Concept of 'Limpieza de Sangre' in Seventeenth-Century Mexico and the Broader Atlantic World," Harvard International Seminar on the History of the Atlantic World, 1500–1800 (April 2002), 2.

10. Martínez uses the work of Paul Gilroy, *The Black Atlantic: Modernity and Double Consciousness* (Cambridge: Harvard University Press, 1993), and others who posit a developing Atlantic culture and worldview. She compares it to historian

Fernand Braudel's Mediterranean world. She is quite aware of the differences between U.S. and British slave economies and Spanish–New Spain economies ("Religion, Purity, and Race," 2–3).

11. Fewer than three, or in some cases, four generations.

12. To the extent that anyone could make that claim, Martínez suggests that the process of creating a national identity for *España Cristiana* required the exclusion of its long multicultural history and a very subjective overemphasis of its Roman and Gothic roots. Martínez, "Religion Purity and Race," 14–16.

13. Martin Bernal, *Black Athena: Afroasiatic Roots of Classical Civilization,* vol. 1, *The Fabrication of Ancient Greece 1785–1985* (New Brunswick, N.J.: Rutgers University Press, 1987).

14. Hannaford, *Race,* 206; see also Bernal, *Black Athena.*

15. Hannaford, *Race,* 208. This evaluation was aesthetic and presupposed that the mean of the continuum of physical appearance was the ideal and that which tended toward either of the extremes of the continuum was less beautiful.

16. Ibid., 211.

17. See Bernal, *Black Athena.*

18. Hannaford, *Race,* 213.

19. Jonathan M. Hess, "Sugar Island Jews? Jewish Emancipation and the Rhetoric of 'Civic Improvement' in Eighteenth Century Germany," *Eighteenth Century Studies* 32, no. 1 (1998) 92–100; and Jonathan M. Hess, "Johann David Michaelis and the Colonial Imaginary: Oriental Studies and the Emergence of Racial Anti-Semitism

in Eighteenth Century Germany," *Jewish Social Studies* 6, no. 2 (winter 2000) 56–101. See also Cornel West, *Prophesy Deliverance! An Afro-American Revolutionary Christianity* (Philadelphia: Westminster, 1982).

20. "AAPA Statement on Biological Aspects of Race," *American Journal of Physical Anthropology* 101 (1996) 569–70.

21. Richard J. Herrnstein and Charles Murray, *The Bell Curve: Intelligence and Class Structure in American Life* (New York: Free Press, 1994).

22. American Anthropological Association, *Statement on "Race" and Intelligence,* December 1994. Available at: http://www.aaanet.org/stmts/race.htm.

2. Race and Religion

1. James H. Cone, *Black Theology and Black Power* (New York: Seabury, 1969).

2. George Lakoff and Mark Johnson, *Philosophy in the Flesh: The Embodied Mind and Its Challenge to Western Thought* (New York: Basic, 1999).

3. Race and the Bible

1. North Americans will understand the analogy of their war, which took place between 1860 and 1864. If one uses the term *Civil War,* it represents one understanding of the conflict; if one refers to the *War between the States,* another connotation is present; while if one refers to the *War of Northern Aggression* or the *War of Southern Secession,* still other organizations of the data are necessary.

2. It is interesting to note that interpreters have had few problems in justifying their choices of referential cultures over the past two hundred years. It seems rather natural to look to contemporary cultures whose direct contacts can be illustrated via similar material cultures, trade routes, linguistic connections, and literary influence and borrowings. It becomes a bit more complicated when one wishes to apply anthropological theories that illustrate connections or possible connections with cultures widely separated by time, space, or both. Nevertheless, this is often the interpreter's best tool for unraveling enigmatic biblical customs that cannot be explained by direct comparisons. Anthropological approaches are not new. As has been shown, they have been used almost since the inception of the historical critical method. Problems have arisen because the assumptions about the validity of early choices of culture have never been challenged. The patterns were set for reasons that seemed logical in the seventeenth century and have never been reexamined. It has been amply demonstrated that many of the decisions made in the early days of the science of anthropology were made in efforts to undergird the then-prevalent assumptions of European superiority based on Christian ideas of divine order. Neither of these ideas retains a place in scientific inquiry today.

3. Jonathan M. Hess, "Sugar Island Jews? Jewish Emancipation and the Rhetoric of 'Civic Improvement' in Eighteenth Century Germany," *Eighteenth Century Studies* 32, no. 1 (1998) 92–100. Hess writes that Michaelis was convinced that such a foundational religious text had its origins in a

magnificent culture such as Egypt's and could be neither Semitic nor African. Apparently it was unimaginable that the forebears of the Jews that Michaelis regarded as absolutely decadent could have developed what he regarded as such high culture.

4. Niels Peter Lemche, "Are We Europeans Really Good Readers of Biblical Texts and Interpreters of Biblical History?" *Journal of Northwest Semitic Languages* 25 (1999) 185–99.

5. C. H. J. van der Merwe, "Hebrew Grammar, Exegesis and Commentaries" *Journal of Northwest Semitic Languages* 11 (1983) 143–56; "A Short Survey of Major Contributions to the Grammatical Description of Old Hebrew Since 1800 A.D.," *Journal of Northwest Semitic Languages* 13 (1987) 161–90; "From Paradigms to Texts: New Horizons and New Tools for Interpreting the Old Testament," *Journal of Northwest Semitic Languages* 22 (1996) 167–79; van der Merwe and W. K. Winkler, "Training Tomorrow's Translators in the Context of Today's Translations," *Journal of Northwest Semitic Languages* 20 (1994) 167–79.

6. Van der Merwe, "From Paradigms to Texts," 176.

7. Often these cultures have been called "primitive."

8. Randall C. Bailey has recently catalogued the types of research being conducted in the United States by African American biblical scholars in his article "Academic Biblical Interpretation among African Americans in the United States," in Vincent L. Wimbush, ed., *African Americans and the Bible: Sacred Texts and Social Textures* (New York:

Continuum, 2001), 696–711. Bailey also provides an appendix of scholars, the institutions in which they earned the doctorates, and their fields of specialization. I take this opportunity to correct a small error in that appendix. My area of specialization is Northwest Semitic Philology, not Hebrew Bible as Bailey indicated. The book *Stony the Road We Trod: African American Biblical Interpretation*, ed. Cain Hope Felder (Minneapolis: Fortress Press, 1991), was hailed as the first academic book published by African American biblical scholars working in cooperation.

9. Frank Yurco, "Egypt and Nubia: Old, Middle and New Kingdom Eras," in *Africa and Africans in Antiquity*, ed. Edwin Yamauchi (East Lansing: Michigan State University Press, 2001), 28–112.

10. See Gene B. Gragg's Afroasiatic Index Project, located at http://www.oi.uchicago.edu/OI/PROJ/CUS/AAindex.html. See also Victor Zinkuratire's "Morphological and Syntactical Similarities between Hebrew and Bantu Languages," *Newsletter on African Old Testament Scholarship* 4 (1998) 4–14.

11. Claus Westermann, *Wurzeln der Weisheit: Die ältesten Sprüche Israels und anderer Völker* (Göttingen: Vandenhoeck & Ruprecht, 1990).

12. Claus Westermann, *Genesis 1–11: A Commentary*, trans. John Scullion, S.J., Continental Commentaries (Minneapolis: Augsburg, 1984), 636.

13. Knut Holter, "The Current State of Old Testament Scholarship in Africa: Where We Are at the Turn of the Century," in *Interpreting the Old Testament in Africa*, ed. Mary N. Getui, Knut Holter, and Victor Zinkuratire (Nairobi: Acton, 2001), 27–39.

14. Charles B. Copher, "The Black Presence in the Old Testament," in Felder, *Stony the Road,* 146–64. A Copher bibliography can be found in the same volume.

15. "The inclusion of Phineas . . . is interesting as providing an independent (and absolutely reliable) confirmation of the tradition that there was a Nubian element in the family of Moses (Num. 12:1)." W. F. Albright, *From Stone Age to Christianity: Monotheism and the Historical Process* (Baltimore: Johns Hopkins University Press, 1946), 193ff., as cited in Copher's article in Felder, *Stony the Road We Trod.*

16. After this section was near its final form, T. N. D. Mettinger directed my attention to "A People Come Out of Egypt: An Egyptologist Looks at the Old Testament," by R. J. Williams, who, with different conclusions about when the contact persisted or was most influential in the development of the Israelite identity, substantially agrees that the influence of Egypt has been undervalued relative to "western Asia." Williams suggests that it is the very nature of Old Testament studies and their natural inclination toward western Asia that has caused this neglect (*Congress Volume: Edinburgh 1974,* Vetus Testamentum Supplements 28 [Leiden: Brill, 1975] 231–52).

17. There is an uncomfortable detail to be sorted out here. After Joseph is betrayed by his brothers, the narrative of Genesis 38 has Judah separating from his brothers to dwell in the land of Adullam (probably Tell esh-Sheikh Madhkur, a bordertown of Judah southwest of Jerusalem). He reappears with the brothers in Genesis 43 as he pleads with Israel to let Benjamin accompany the

other ten in their return to Egypt to seek food during the famine.

18. Maricel Mena López, "Raizes afro-asiaticas nas origens do povo de Israel," Ph.D. dissertation, Universidade Metodista de Sao Paulo, May 7, 2002.

19. The same phenomenon is recorded concerning the recently freed African Americans who exited slavery in the eighteenth century. Likewise it is often cited as a lack of competence or readiness for emancipation and therefore a negative characteristic, but not usually as rebellion against the Creator. In both cases, it is reasonable to consider a mixture of emotions that include a sense of loss of the familiar and even some parts of the relationships with those who had regarded themselves as the lords over their own lives and labor. If these emotions were not mixed, neither the Hebrews nor African Americans would be full humans.

20. Randall Bailey, Charles Copher, and, to a different degree, Frank Snowden. See, for example, Randall C. Bailey, "Beyond Identification: The Use of Africans in Old Testament Poetry and Narratives," in Felder, *Stony the Road,* 165–84; and Frank M. Snowden Jr., *Blacks in Antiquity: Ethiopians in the Greco-Roman Experience* (Cambridge, Mass.: Belknap, 1970) and *Before Color Prejudice: The Ancient View of Blacks* (Cambridge: Harvard University Press, 1983).

21. Martin Noth, *The Old Testament World,* trans. Victor I. Gruhn (Philadelphia: Fortress Press, 1966); W. F. Albright, "The Old Testament World," in *The Interpreter's Bible,* 12 vols., ed. G. A. Buttrick (New York: Abingdon-Cokesbury, 1951–57), 1:233–71.

22. I have already intimated above that the physical evidence can be compared for anthropological (archaeological) evidence of shared culture. Here I mean to emphasize new approaches that have not typically been used and, to my knowledge, almost never used in the West to consider possible ties between biblical and African cultural practices.

23. James H. Cone, *Black Theology and Black Power* (New York: Seabury, 1969). Later, in *Spirituals and the Blues: An Interpretation* (New York: Seabury, 1972), he would associate the need to sing the blues with this social stratum turned racial group.

24. After a long history, which continues today, of hearing *black* and *dark* used as negative images, Cone managed to reverse this trend and, at least in a determined part of the world of theology, bring forth the understanding that God could see black as a positive part of creation.

Bibliography

Albright, W. F. "The Old Testament World." In *The Interpreter's Bible*. 12 vols. Edited by G. A. Buttrick, 1:233–71. New York: Abingdon-Cokesbury, 1951–57.

Bailey, Randall C. "Academic Biblical Interpretation among African Americans in the United States." In *African Americans and the Bible: Sacred Texts and Social Textures,* edited by Vincent L. Wimbush, 696–711. New York: Continuum, 2001.

———. "Beyond Identification: The Use of Africans in Old Testament Poetry and Narratives." In *Stony the Road We Trod: African American Biblical Interpretation,* ed. Cain Hope Felder, 165–84. Minneapolis: Fortress Press, 1991.

Bernal, Martin. *Black Athena: Afroasiatic Roots of Classical Civilization*. Vol. 1: *The Fabrication of Ancient Greece 1785–1985*. New Brunswick, N.J.: Rutgers University Press, 1987.

Cone, James H. *Black Theology and Black Power*. New York: Seabury, 1969.

———. *Spirituals and the Blues: An Interpretation*. New York: Seabury, 1972.

Copher, Charles B. "The Black Presence in the Old Testament." In *Stony the Road,* 146–64.

Felder, Cain Hope, ed. *Stony the Road We Trod: African American Biblical Interpretation.* Minneapolis: Fortress Press, 1991.

Gilroy, Paul. *The Black Atlantic: Modernity and Double Consciousness.* Cambridge: Harvard University Press, 1993.

Hannaford, Ivan. *Race: The History of an Idea in the West.* Baltimore: Johns Hopkins University Press, 1996.

Hess, Jonathan M. "Johann David Michaelis and the Colonial Imaginary: Oriental Studies and the Emergence of Racial Anti-Semitism in Eighteenth Century Germany." *Jewish Social Studies* 6/2 (winter 2000) 56–101.

———. "Sugar Island Jews? Jewish Emancipation and the Rhetoric of 'Civic Improvement' in Eighteenth Century Germany." *Eighteenth Century Studies* 32/1 (1998) 92–100.

Holter, Knut. "The Current State of Old Testament Scholarship in Africa: Where We Are at the Turn of the Century." In *Interpreting the Old Testament in Africa,* edited by Mary N. Getui, Knut Holter, and Victor Zinkuratire, 27–39. Nairobi: Acton, 2001.

Lakoff, George, and Mark Johnson. *Philosophy in the Flesh: The Embodied Mind and Its Challenge to Western Thought.* New York: Basic, 1999.

Lemche, Niels Peter. "Are We Europeans Really Good Readers of Biblical Texts and Interpreters of Biblical History?" *Journal of Northwest Semitic Languages* 25 (1999) 185–99.

Lévi-Strauss, Claude. *Race and History.* The Race Question in Modern Science. Paris: UNESCO, 1952.

Martínez, María Elena. "Religion, Purity, and Race: The Spanish Concept of 'Limpieza de Sangre' in Seventeenth-Century Mexico and the Broader Atlantic World." Harvard International Seminar on the History of the Atlantic World, 1500–1800, April 2002.

Noth, Martin. *The Old Testament World.* Trans. Victor I. Gruhn. Philadelphia: Fortress Press, 1966.

Snowden, Frank M., Jr. *Before Color Prejudice: The Ancient View of Blacks.* Cambridge: Harvard University Press, 1983.

——. *Blacks in Antiquity: Ethiopians in the Greco-Roman Experience.* Cambridge, Mass.: Belknap, 1970.

Tanner, Kathryn. *Theories of Culture: A New Agenda for Theology.* Guides to Theological Inquiry. Minneapolis: Fortress Press, 1997.

van der Merwe, C. H. J. "Hebrew Grammar, Exegesis, and Commentaries." *Journal of Northwest Semitic Languages* 11 (1983) 143–56.

——. "A Short Survey of Major Contributions to the Grammatical Description of Old Hebrew Since 1800 A.D.," *Journal of Northwest Semitic Languages* 13 (1987) 161–90.

——. "Training Tomorrow's Translators in the Context of Today's Translations," *Journal of Northwest Semitic Languages* 20 (1994) 167–79.

van der Merwe, C. H. J., and W. K. Winkler, "From Paradigms to Texts: New Horizons and New Tools for Interpreting the Old Testament." *Journal of Northwest Semitic Languages* 22 (1996) 167–79.

Westermann, Claus. *Genesis 1–11: A Commentary.* Translated by John Scullion, S.J. Continental Commentaries. Minneapolis: Augsburg, 1984.

———. *Wurzeln der Weisheit: Die ältesten Sprüche Israels und anderer Völker.* Göttingen: Vandenhoeck & Ruprecht, 1990.

Williams, R. J. "A People Come Out of Egypt: An Egyptologist Looks at the Old Testament," *Congress Volume: Edinburgh 1974,* 231–52. Vetus Testamentum Supplements 28. Leiden: Brill, 1975.

Wimbush, Vincent L., ed. *African Americans and the Bible: Sacred Texts and Social Textures.* New York: Continuum, 2001.

Yurco, Frank. "Egypt and Nubia: Old, Middle and New Kingdom Eras." In *Africa and Africans in Antiquity,* edited by Edwin Yamauchi, 28–112. East Lansing: Michigan State University Press, 2001.